8 THINGS
MY PARENTS
DIDN'T TELL ME
ABOUT MONEY

8 THINGS MY PARENTS DIDN'T TELL ME ABOUT MONEY

Young America's Guide to Financial and Personal Success

Odell A. Bizzell II

The more money you have, the more people you can help.

Distributed by:

Impact Intellectual Properties

P.O. Box 5094

Greensboro, NC 27435

ISBN #: 978-1-490-52784-0

Most if not all of your dreams and goals can be achieved more easily with the aid of lots of money

Learn How to Help Your Student Graduate Debt Free and Have $10,000 in the bank by 25 with these Free Financial Success Videos Here:

www.ImpactStudentFinances.com

Dedication

"Beloved, I pray that in all things thou mayest prosper and be in health, even as thy soul prospereth." 3 John 1:2

I give all honor and glory to my GOD and my divine power for all that is inside of me. I'm so grateful for my beautiful wife, Sierra, and my children, Makayla, Raine, and Will. The first edition of this book didn't include their names because they had not yet been born.

To you reading this, this is the second edition of this book. The first edition was written back in 2011. And after thousands of copies sold, along with thousands of lives touched, I assure you this iteration of this book will be even more impactful than the first.

If you set a goal to make more money honorably than you ever thought possible, then you make a goal to touch more people and become more valuable than you ever thought possible.

Contents

Make it a necessity to be extraordinary financially.

Learn How to Help Your Student Graduate Debt Free and Have $10,000 in the bank by 25 with these Free Financial Success Videos Here:

www.ImpactStudentFinances.com

The More Things Change

A LOT HAS CHANGED SINCE the first edition of this book was released. I have two more children than I had before, I'm ten years older, and social media has made the world a smaller place. This book and many of my others have been read by tens of thousands of people all across the country and beyond. A lot has changed, but as the old saying goes: "The more things change, the more they stay the same." Despite all of the changes that have ensued over the last decade, money is still very important.

Most people's top three list of most important things in life include GOD, family, and then probably money, usually in that order. However, I believe you would agree with me in saying that the first two things are affected greatly by the third. If you believe in GOD and attend church there is a time where the church solicits funds from the members by way of tithes and offering, and if you are struggling to pay your bills it's very difficult to honor GOD with money you don't have.

Subsequently, if you have a demanding job or a job that doesn't pay well, you are either away from your family more than you like or you cannot make ends meet with your current paycheck which are both quandaries that no one wants. All in all, we know that money affects a multitude of things outside of dollars and cents.

So what does that have to do with you reading this book? Well, I don't know about you, but when I was younger my parents were able to give me pretty much everything I needed, but the extra stuff was out of the question. This book will help young people and their parents better understand the third most important thing in most people's lives, money.

I remember back in high school when I wanted a pair of black and gray Nike shox. Back then that particular pair of shoes was about $150, and at that point I was a star on my varsity basketball team and some of my fellow teammates were getting the newest shoes, so I approached my mom with the opportunity to purchase the new Nikes for me. She respectfully declined, stating and I quote, "$150 for a pair of shoes? I could pay the light bill and put gas in the car with that much money.

You must think money grows outside on one of those trees in the backyard!" But my hope wasn't totally crushed because after her rant she said that if I could come up with half of the money she would buy the shoes for me. She did not, however, tell me how to come up with the other half.

Though it wasn't what I wanted to hear, the little rant my mom gave set me on a quest that day. From that day on I was obsessed with creating money so I could buy more stuff. Shortly after that, I started selling candy out of my backpack to my classmates at school. Then things started getting interesting. As the demand for my product increased I added my friend Justin to the mix and then we started to take over candy distribution at Ben L. Smith High School.

By our senior year, we had earned over $75,000 selling candy to classmates. From that experience I learned a few things about business and developed a hunger for becoming a business owner.

As a student at NC State, I was set on owning a business and through my father I was able to meet a wealthy mentor who offered to teach me to become a business owner. I halfway listened to my mentor and was able to purchase a barbershop and a vending machine route at nineteen. Since I had so much success early on I felt as if I didn't need my mentor's advice anymore, so after my first two commercial business purchases, I stopped seeking his guidance.

Now, if I were to stop the story there then that would be an awesome success story; but the story does not end there. If you notice earlier in this chapter I said that I was "obsessed with creating money so I could buy more stuff" and I also said that I "halfway listened to my mentor." The rest of the story isn't so great.

Though I would love to tell you that after that early business success, I became more savvy and was able to turn that small fortune into a Fortune 500 corporation that currently employs 1,000 people, I can't. What actually happened was I became very prideful and greedy. Pride and greed lead to a great fall and my fall was very painful. I was a college student on a full academic scholarship my freshman year and did not take my studies seriously and lost my scholarship and then had to get student loans.

I got the maximum amount of private student loans I could get because I believed that with the extra money I could buy more businesses and once I got out of college, three long years later, that I would easily be able to pay off the student loans in full without a problem. Well things didn't exactly go like that; in fact, they didn't go anything like that. I began getting involved with get rich quick scams that Bernie Madoff would've laughed at and ended up selling my businesses to get involved with risky stock investments.

By the end of my senior year, I was an average student, with no businesses, no money, no resume for a job, and no job prospects. I graduated from NC State with a degree and no clue. No clue on how to become financially successful and I was faced with the reality that no money in the real world is no joke. So what happened to me after that? I licked my wounds, got a job as a detention officer at the local jail and went back to study under my mentor. I will never forget the conversation we had.

"You got greedy, didn't you?" he said, giving me that half smile he always gave me. "Yeah I did, I got greedy and stupid. I thought I knew it all," I said sadly, not even looking up. He responded in a way that surprised me. "Well, at least you were stupid and greedy at twenty-two and not forty-two. That's your first lesson, most people can't be stupid, greedy, and rich," he said walking toward his desk. He sat behind his desk and stated the reason I wrote this book over ten years ago.

"I want you to be wealthy. Odell, I want to ask you a question and I don't want to offend you in any way, but are your parents wealthy?" he said, staring me in the eyes with a stoic look. I thought to myself and attempted to find the "trick" in the question.

Did he mean wealthy as in: do my parents have lots of money and don't work? Or did he mean are my parents wealthy like they have lots of money and high paying jobs? "What exactly do you mean by wealthy?" I asked, seeking more clarification. "I mean if your parents lost their jobs could they maintain their standard of living for an infinite amount of time," he responded.

"No not at all, they'd probably pass out and have a conniption or something," I said laughing. "Though that is probably true, your answer is very telling. If your parents are not wealthy, or not even financially savvy, how could they teach you to be?" At that moment, I quickly reviewed my short business career and discovered that it was showered with terrible financial mistakes.

If I had simply saved most of the money I made from my candy business in high school, learned more about the barbershop and vending businesses, maybe I would've done better. But I always spent everything I made for the most part and so did my parents. Now I am not blaming my parents, but I believe that if we knew better, we would do better.

My parents taught me good morals and ethics because they practiced them, they didn't teach me great financial skills because they weren't taught those things. From that point on, my mentor told me that he would personally teach me to be wealthy, as long as I stayed humble and hungry. He gave me eight principles you hold in your hands that will truly unlock your financial future. Since I've implemented these principles in my life, I've been able to overcome seemingly insurmountable student loan debt, have a thriving career as a nationally known professional speaker, meet and work with celebrities, and start creating a financial future that most people only dream of.

I am not writing this book as a guru on finance, an expert on wealth, or anything of that nature. Consider me a happy messenger passing on the message of prosperity to young people. No one can go back in time and change the decisions they made, but I believe if I can help someone still in school learn a few things that I didn't know about money, I can change their future.

And if you are a parent or an older person you can learn from these principles as well because though I am screaming at the younger generation, these principles are timeless and can work for anybody willing to implement them. This book is short and to the point and I assure you if it is read and studied it will provide great information for anyone trying to have a successful financial life. Many of the things my mentor told me about money were very simple and obvious and left me saying, "I think I got it now!" And I am confident you will have the same reaction!

Since 2011, when I first published this book, so much has changed in the world and in my life. Social media was not even close to what it is now. Society in the 2020s and beyond was very different and because of that, I want you to understand something: We live in a capitalistic society.

Don't lament that fact, but rather take advantage of it. Make it a goal to have more than enough. Make it a goal to be wealthy. Don't settle for being comfortable. Don't be afraid to succeed because others never will. Money is not the only measure of success, but it is a major one. Embrace it, be successful and happy reading! Also this book comes with an accompanying video series where I'm interviewing financial experts and people that have done well financially based on the principles in this book and beyond.

All you have to do is sign up with your name and email at www.ImpactStudentFinances.com and then just watch out for the interviews and content delivered straight to your inbox. Enjoy the book and I can't wait to hear about your success.

****

**Learn How to Help Your Student Graduate
Debt Free and Have $10,000 in the bank by 25
with these Free Financial Success Videos Here:**

www.ImpactStudentFinances.com

CHAPTER 1:

Make Financial Success a Necessity

THE LESSONS WITH MY MENTOR started in his home every week. He would always give me great insight along with an assignment. He started our first session with a very powerful point. "It's tough becoming wealthy, Odell, it took me about fifteen years to get where I am, so the first thing you need to understand is that **if you are going to become financially successful you have to make it a need not a want.**"

Think about that. Most people say that they only *need* to graduate from college and get a job that will pay them enough to cover their basic needs. Consequently, what usually ends up happening is that people get what they need and that's it. **Believe that having lots of money and obtaining lots of assets with passive income is just as necessary as getting a job.** You need to believe it's necessary to have lots of money like it's necessary to eat. Just like you believe it's necessary to eat that pizza at lunch time, I need you to believe

1

it's necessary to have lots of money.

This book is a guide to financial achievement for the young people in America. What you have to understand is that **it is better to be financially successful than it is to be broke**. This seems elementary, but the only way you're going to believe it is if it's simple. Furthermore, a lot of people grow up believing that they can't be good and giving people and make a lot of money. This is false and I know you'll see the holes in that logic after reading this book.

There are three basic reasons why you should believe financial success is a necessity: (1) The rules of money have changed, (2) Money gives you options, and (3) You will live a better life.

The first reason you have to believe financial success is a necessity is because the rules have changed. There was once a point in time when you could go to college, graduate, and go to work for a company and all while you worked, that company put money away for you. So after 30-40 years you would have hundreds of thousands of dollars possibly millions, put away for retirement. In short, the company took care of your financial future so you didn't have to worry much about it. And this way of life is still being sold today.

For most people however, it's not a sustainable way of living life financially. You have to secure your own financial future. If you don't properly plan for your financial future then you cannot expect to have a bright financial future. If you start now, you can easily be financially successful through investments and other avenues far before you get older. Your mindset about creating financial freedom is very important, but I want to challenge you not to only plan to build wealth by retirement age which is over sixty, but far before that.

One of the biggest reasons you should make it a necessity to become financially successful is because **having money gives you more options in life.** When you get out of high school and college, money will be the driving force of your survival, if it's not already. Those who are financially successful have the option to choose the vacations they want to go on, what time they want to wake up in the morning, how much they want to spend for holidays, and so on. Don't you want those options for your life?

Imagine being able to go to the mall and buy something without cringing at the price or worrying whether or not you are going to overdraft your bank account. Don't you want the freedom to make decisions based on what you want and what's best for you? And let's go a little deeper than that. You have access to information and opportunities that not even your parents could have dreamed of having. It is your obligation to turn this access into success so that more people can access their success and be happier.

When you are bound by only a salary from a job, your earning potential is limited. Moreover, when you have lots of money you can decide what you want to do with your time. **Your time is the most valuable asset you have.** Don't you want to be able to spend your time in the manner you want to spend it? You can not only spend your time how you want to, but with more money you have the option to give more of yourself.

You have the option to give more money and more time to causes you believe in and people that need your help in this world. I am currently updating this book while the world is going through a global pandemic. People have lost jobs, opportunities, businesses, and the like. It's been a tragedy. What this pandemic has taught me is the value in having low debt and multiple streams of income. I was one of the fortunate ones that didn't have to stop my business; in fact, my business grew during the pandemic.

But I also understand that I got the lessons you are about to read when I was in my early twenties. If you're reading this and you're a teenager, you need to thank the person who gave you this book. If you're older reading this book just to make sure it's sound information for a young person you care about, grab a hold to the principles that make sense to you.

As a financially free adult, you will have the option to spend your money and time serving others and your family. All in all, you do not have to be bound by a boss or someone telling you when to come and when to go, what to wear, and what to do. Financially successful people have the option to freely show the world the good they have to offer them.

Finally, financial success is a necessity because you will live a better life. Your quality of life will be greatly expanded if you are financially successful. You will be able to afford the best quality food so you will be healthier, you will be able to afford the best insurance, the best cars, the best clothes, and live in the best neighborhoods. Financial success affords you the best, and isn't that what we all want? Don't you want the best for yourself, and your family?

Make financial success a necessity to set a higher level of expectation for your life. I love what legendary speaker Les Brown says, *"Most people don't fail in life because they shoot too high and miss, but rather because they shoot too low and hit it every time."* Financial success is something that most people don't achieve in their life because they don't shoot for it. I want to repeat something I heard my mentor say to me one time: If you had all the money in the world what *couldn't* you do?

Let me also add that financial success isn't about the car you drive, it's about being driven to achieve something that has never been done in your family history. Financial success isn't about the house you live in, but it's about having the option to create the type of home you want to have.

Financial success isn't about what you have in your bank account; it's about having the freedom to give of yourself however you want without financial pressure. Make financial success a necessity in your life and you won't regret it; on the other hand, don't make financial success a necessity and risk being financially mediocre forever.

****

Chapter 1:
Things to Do

- Define financial success for you and write it down.
- Identify five reasons why you should be financially successful.
- Identify five people that would benefit from your financial success.
- Sign up for the video series at **www.ImpactStudentFinances.com** and watch the video connected to this chapter.

Chapter 2:

Invest in Yourself

When I was twenty years old, I attended a seminar that changed my life forever. I was working a summer job for my mentor's financial services company and they brought a speaker in to speak at their national convention, his name was Myron Golden. It was the most electrifying, exciting, amazing presentation I had ever seen. There is a lot of information from that seminar that I still use in my life today.

Myron said so many great things in his speech that I would like to use this chapter to share some of them with you. His theme was that most people do not become financially successful because they do not put enough money in their own personal development. Personal development is the conscious effort of becoming the best person you can be in all aspects of life and finances is one of those aspects.

When you practice personal development you take out the time and money to develop more skills, a better philosophy on life, and more applicable knowledge to use to move you further along in life. My mentor told me something I want to share with you:

"Odell, you can tell a lot about what people value by what they spend money on." **The person that spends the most money on consumer items cares more about their present than their future**. If you want to separate yourself and become wealthy, you have to spend more money and time on your personal development than you do anything else.

Benjamin Franklin echoes my mentor's sentiments with his quote, *"Empty your purse into your mind, and your mind will fill your purse with gold."* I love Ben Franklin's quotes because they are so simple but so profound and they come with simple instructions to follow. If you want to be financially successful, you have to invest in your own personal development. Invest in purchasing books, audios, and mentors that will teach you things that will put you ahead in the future.

I understand how difficult it is to look to the future when you're young. I remember being a teenager and people in their thirties and forties talking that old people talk, saying things like: "Back in my day…" or "If I only knew then, what I know now," and so on and so forth.

But those who invest in themselves the earliest are the ones that will achieve the highest heights. I have literally spent tens of thousands of dollars for seminars, books, audio series, and financial education. That's one of the main reasons I am where I am financially.

I am not saying that you have to spend thousands to begin to grow financially. The fact that you are reading this book right now is an example of investing in yourself. I am saying, however, there must be a sacrifice of resources and time to grow. Reading and buying more books on financial education, marketing, leadership, entrepreneurship, and other skills are essential to becoming financially successful.

The late Charlie "Tremendous" Jones, the hall of fame speaker and world-renowned motivator said, *"You will be the same person today that you will be five years from now except for two things: the people you hang around and the books that you read."* Now what if that's true? In five years you could be anything you dreamed of being if you read the right things and hung around the right people. My suggestion is try it out!

My challenge to you is for you to add five years to your age and look at what you want to become by that age. So if you are seventeen and by age twenty-two you want to have a college degree, $10,000 saved, and own a business, you need to feverishly be investing in books, audios, and people that will help you get there. The same goes for those individuals who are older. Discover how you want to live in five years and invest in yourself by finding the right people and the right books to read to live that lifestyle.

What usually happens with many people is they want a lot, but never invest money and time in their self-education and self motivation. **You need to make a habit of reading books and listening to people that have value on subjects that will move you toward your financial goals.**

The more people pay for something, the more value they perceive it has. Which pair of shoes is better: a pair of Jordans or Adidas? If you do not invest in yourself, then in your mind, you will not feel like you deserve to do better financially. The main reason you should invest in yourself is so that you can become more valuable. By spending time and money on your own self-education, you will learn more about things to propel you to financial heights.

Famous author Mark Twain said, *"A formal education will make you a living, an informal education will make you a fortune."* Your informal education is what you learn outside of school. You see, education without application is no education at all. Education is designed to move us forward. Most people only learn stuff in the classroom and don't ever go outside of school to learn what school doesn't teach. Properly educating yourself will teach you how to make a fortune. If you only learn how to pass Algebra and get your diploma, you will limit your earning power.

I want to give you an example. Let's say two people go to college and graduate with 4.0 GPAs and get jobs paying $50,000/year. If one of the people learns how to start their own business by attending seminars and reading books and the other doesn't, which one do you think has the potential to be better off quicker?

Note that they won't be better off financially because they are smarter or more talented, but simply because they decided to invest in themselves. **The most precious gift you can give the world is a bigger better you**. Begin working harder on yourself than you do on anything else and you will be better for it. What stops most people from going to the next level is the fact that they don't spend enough money or time on their self education.

First, invest time in setting goals. My mentor told me that I should have a date with my future by taking time everyday (yes everyday) working on my ideal scene. Your ideal scene is what you want your life to look like on a daily basis in the future. For example, a simple ideal scene in your life could be that in fifteen years you want to have over $20,000 in the bank, own three rental homes, be married, live in a $200,000 home and have a monthly passive income of $4,000 from real estate and businesses. Take time developing this ideal scene then get the tools to achieve it.

You should also invest time in studying for what you want. **Success is the consistent study of the obvious.** If you have the aforementioned goals, you have to study on how to get them. I once heard that if you wish to have happiness you should study happiness, and if you wish to be wealthy you should study wealth. So if you want to achieve your goals then study them.

The second thing you should invest in yourself is money. What is awesome about investing money in yourself is you do not have to spend a whole lot of money to achieve great results. This book cost about $20, and you will expand your horizons and understand how to achieve great things in your life. So make a habit of buying books, audios, and other things that don't cost a whole lot of money, but offer great value. One chapter of a book can change your life.

This is why I wrote this book. I have done a lot of positive things financially in my life, but had my parents known to teach me a better way, I would be better off. That's my hope for you. **My hope is that you will live the life of your dreams, and the only way to do that is to spend money and time investing in yourself.**

The Magic of Compound Interest

In addition to investing money and time in yourself it is also wise to study the stock market and a concept called compound in-terest. I want to quote a few really famous guys from the past, one of which you've already heard me quote. First, Ben Franklin said: **"Life's tragedy is that we get old too soon, and wise too late."** The next person I want to quote is one of the most famous minds in the history of mankind, Albert Einstein who said, **"Compound interest is the eighth wonder of the world, he who understands it, earns it ... he who doesn't ... pays it."**

Here's what both of those quotes mean to you and your financial future. My mentor was a millionaire in his forties and he was teaching me in my twenties. He told me one time during one of our sessions: "Youth is wasted on the young and wisdom is less useful as you age." You will hear this multiple times: **financial success is developed over time**. My grandma retired at the age of sixty, I was 6 years old. Most of my life she's been retired and it all started with her putting aside $25 a month.

Because my grandmother is almost ninety years old, let's adjust the numbers for modern times. If you put $100 a month away starting at the age of twenty, let's see what that means. If at the age of twenty you put $100 into an investment account and only contributed $100 a month, by the time you turned forty years old you would have $55,380.45 in an investment account (assuming an 8 percent annual interest rate).

If you continued doing this until you turned sixty you would have over $313,000 in an account. And that's just from $100 a month with an 8 percent annual return. That shows the power of compound interest over time. If you invest more money and even more wisely it could be a lot more. The point of this illustration is that being young you need to be figuring out how to multiply your efforts over time. The stock market can do that for you, but you must first work on your own personal development. You only deserve wealth if you put in the work over a long period of time. Invest in yourself and your financial betterment and it will pay off.

****

Chapter 2:
Things to Do

- Develop written financial and personal goals.
- Finish reading this book, and read one book a month!
- Make a goal of spending AT LEAST fifteen minutes a day studying something that will help you achieve your goals.
- Sign up for the video series at **www.ImpactStudentFinances.com** and watch the video connected to this chapter.

CHAPTER 3:

You Need Profits & Wages

IN ORDER TO BECOME WEALTHY you must have profits and wages. In other words you need some kind of sustainable income stream before you get a risky one. Sometimes seeing someone young and successful throws you off. You begin comparing where they are to where you think you should be. That leads you down a path of expectation without sacrifice.

Everyone who has achieved great wealth has given up something that most people know nothing about. This book is not about you creating a fortune out of thin air. It's about making sure that you're successful and wealthy no matter what, which leads me to the third lesson. At your age and station in life **you should strive to obtain profits and wages until your profits greatly outweigh your expenses.**

As a teenager you need to have fun and enjoy your youth, but you can do that and still make money! When I got to middle school I was like most teenagers in America, my parents paid for my necessities.

However, once I got to high school my mindset changed. I was in the ninth grade playing varsity basketball and hanging around upperclassmen and I wanted to do some of the things they were doing. I wanted to be able to buy the shoes I wanted, see the movies I wanted, and take my girlfriend to the nicest restaurants. So I started selling candy for some extra money.

My parents continued paying for everything I needed, so all the money I made was straight profit. If I had had the wherewithal to get a job on top of that I would have had even more money. Money is important, start earning profits and wages as soon as you can. We'll discuss this again, but profits are money from a business and wages are money from a job. One includes your time, the other doesn't always include just your time but we'll discuss that a little later.

Once you begin working for your own money, you will appreciate it more which will help you better manage it.

How Do You Win the Game of Monopoly?

Most people have heard of the legendary board game Monopoly. A lot of people have played the game. I've asked thousands of teenagers this question throughout the countless times I've given presentations based on this book: *How do you win the game of Monopoly?*

I've heard lots of different answers over the years. These are some of the most common ones: "Take everybody's money!" "Make everyone go bankrupt!" I would also get a laundry list of complaints about the game being too long, boring, and a bit pointless. All those years ago when I was giving my mentor some of these exact same answers to the how-do-you-win-the-game-of-Monopoly question, he revealed to me two things that I want to convey to you.

The first was about mindset. Financial success is more about goal setting and discipline than it is about money. Setting goals and being disciplined is all about money. He went on to say, "Odell, when you sit down and play Monopoly you have to know the rules and be disciplined to follow them. Most people don't know the rules of Monopoly and don't understand how they can make the rules work for them."

The last part of that previous sentence is important to note. 'Most people don't understand how they can make the rules work for them.' There are standard rules, but you can also create house rules. In other words, you can create rules to help you win. An example of a house rule is creating an objective for the game. You can say that you will play until the first person goes around the board twenty times and whoever has amassed the most cash or net worth at that time wins the game.

That's an example of being creative with the game of Monopoly. Instead, most people complain: "Monopoly lasts too long, that's why we don't play!" Just make the game shorter.

The second thing I want to address that my mentor taught me as it relates to Monopoly and profits and wages is this: How you win the game. Another rule a lot of people misinterpret is how to win the game. In relation to how you win the game, most people answered the same way I did earlier on. But no matter how many people I've asked this question, they've never answered this way: "You win the game of Monopoly by going around the board as many times as you can, passing 'Go,' collecting $200, saving your money without investing it."

That's key. I hope you didn't miss it. Monopoly is a game about building wealth, period. Your goal in the game is to become wealthy. Just in case you missed my point about collecting and saving, let me emphasize the point by adding this: If that's not how you win the game of Monopoly, which is a game about building wealth, then why are we taught to do that in real life? That's how most people play the money game and that's why they lose.

They hope to collect the highest salaries they can find and by some stroke of stock market magic or a lottery moment that they make a lot of money. This is faulty thinking at best. **Monopoly teaches us we need wages starting out and as we properly invest our wages we can build great profits.** How do you go about earning wages and profits?

Let's start with wages. A wage is income you earn via a job. You are exchanging time for money when you earn a wage. Don't worry about this early on because when you're young, odds are you have more time and fewer responsibilities. If you are sixteen years of age or older then you can legally apply for a job without parental consent. If you are fifteen you can apply for a worker's permit and go to work with your parent's permission. **I am an advocate for wealth, but before most get wealth you need to be able to have an income that sustains your livelihood.**

No matter your situation, apply to all the jobs you can and begin earning a wage early on. Be the best employee that you can be, and learn how the business you are working in operates. **There are two primary reasons you should get a job, the first reason is to create income, but the second reason is so you can learn how a business runs and operates.**

Profits can be earned via a business or self employment venture. This is what I did at fourteen, and if I had read a book like this I would have gotten an after school job to make even more money. All teenagers should start an opportunity where they can make extra money. I believe this is the best way to begin creating profits because, though you need profits and wages, over time profits are better than wages. You earn wages on a job; you earn profits through self employment or a business.

The reason profits are better than wages is because wages are paid based on time. If you work a certain number of hours on a job then you will get paid a certain amount of money or wage. Profits can be accumulated even when you are not physically working, with the right system, and are usually made via a product sale or a service rendered.

Let's say for example you started selling special SAT study guides online for $20 a guide. The time it takes you to develop the study guide, build the website, and start marketing to all your friends and others is a total of forty hours.

After that you wouldn't have to do anymore "work" outside of marketing the guides. If you sold 100 SAT study guides in one month you would make $2,000 for forty hours of work. If you had a job that paid you $7 per hour you would have to work 285 hours to make that same $2,000 and then you would be taxed on it right then and there. Do you see why profits can be better than wages? **To earn profits you have to work more up front, but you get paid more on the back end, and you spend less of your time working for the money in most cases.**

Profits can be multiplied and wages can only be added to. The simple message is: start earning profits *and* wages while you are young and don't have a lot of responsibilities. The sooner you begin earning income the sooner you will begin learning the value of money and the sooner you can begin accumulating money for the future.

I am not telling you to start earning money so you can spend it all on "stuff" I am saying that you should start earning money now so that you can learn what it's like to earn money and so you can have some later on.

When you actually earn something by working for it you begin to cherish it all the more; when it is given to you, your appreciation for it is limited. When you have an abundance of money it's easier for you to invest in yourself and start learning how to multiply money. It's very difficult to buy a book for $15 if you don't have the money to buy it! But that book may show you how to turn $100 into $1,000.

If you want to get a part-time job the best places to get one are restaurants, country clubs, grocery stores, your local mall, and movie theatres. I know these places don't sound glamorous, but they will hire people with little to no experience. The summertime is a great time to find a job as well, but don't wait until you are out of school, start working weekends during the school year and then once the summer starts you can already be on staff so you won't have to compete with all the other people trying to get seasonal jobs.

Another way to get a job is to find someone who has their own business and work for them doing odd jobs and just busy work. Examples of this are working with an accountant and helping out during tax season, you could help a landscaper out cutting grass, you can sweep up hair at a barbershop on the weekends. If you wanted to start an opportunity there are a lot of things that you could do. I want to give you a short list of things that you can do if you want to start your own opportunity, or your own business.

These are just examples of things that you could do that could produce income for you quickly. You may or may not find these beneficial, but hopefully they will start the wheels in your head to turn a little bit:

- Yard work/Cut grass
- Babysit
- Do makeup
- Host monthly bake sales
- Fix computers
- Real estate scouting
- Do taxes
- Start a membership of some kind
- Dog walk/Dog sit
- Cut hair/Do hair
- Give pedicures
- Get a sales job
- Fix cars
- Tutor
- Do odd jobs
- Online business

A few of those items may not make sense to you, such as real estate scouting, starting a membership, or an online business, but that's why it is important to visit **www.ImpactStudentFinances. com** and join our email list and watch the videos connected to this book. I go deeper into creating money making opportunities that few people would think about.

But just look at the items above and let your mind begin to create more and more ideas to generate money and act on the ones you like the most.

My simple message to you is, again, begin creating income as soon as possible, but understand you need both profits and wages.

Working for your money teaches you that you cannot ever get anything worth getting without working hard at it. This is a universal law; **you cannot get something for nothing**.

Lots of people believe that financial success will come to them just because they pray, wish, or hope for it. People pray that they win the lottery, their son or daughter is a famous mega superstar, or someone they didn't know they were related to dies and leaves them a million dollars. **Don't let your financial success hinge on a wish and a prayer.** If you begin doing things now to create income, you open yourself up to so many opportunities because you are learning skills.

If you are not yet sold on a business or earning profits then I want you to hear what my mentor told me when we discussed this lesson. "Odell, if you were to study the fortunes of 1,000 millionaires, I guarantee you that over 990 of them obtained their wealth from a business of some kind. So what does that tell you?" he asked. "Naturally if I want to be a millionaire, I need to own a business, right?" I said.

"Absolutely, and it also tells you that profits are better than wages when looking to become financially successful, but you need both in the beginning. It's a tougher road in the beginning, but after you make it, it's smooth sailing."

****

Chapter 3:
Things to Do

- Write out a list of days you can work during the school year and how many hours you can work.

- Find a job working for a company or working with someone to begin creating income and/or start your own opportunity using your own ideas or some of the ones provided in this lesson.

- Sign up for the video series at **www.ImpactStudentFinances.com** and watch the video connected to this chapter.

Your goal in life should be to have enough money so that you can be a full-time servant to your creator and your purpose.

CHAPTER 4:

Live on Half of What You Make

BEFORE THIS LESSON STARTED, I asked my mentor what he would do to build his fortune if he were starting over. "That's easy. Let's say I was in your shoes--twenty-two years old, no job, and I am living with my parents. The first thing I would do is get a job, the second thing I would do is begin working on the side in real estate. The third thing I would do is actually our lesson for today and that is, I would live on half of what I made." What a concept!

Simple math will make you wealthy. If you make $3,000 a month on your job and only need $1,500 to live on, you can save $18,000 a year. After that first year you can buy real estate; begin investing in the stock market, or other businesses, until your passive income (i.e. your profits) are greater than your expenses. Getting your passive income from assets to bring in more money than you need to live a comfortable and enjoyable life is the goal.

Then you can move on to making really big money. It all starts with being disciplined, having a plan to become financially success-ful, and living on half of what you make. Ultimately, you want to play Monopoly in real life. Meaning: the half of the money you don't need to live on you begin to invest. **Wealth is built over a period**

of time, longer than most desire, but shorter than most expect.

In a special video that can be found after you sign up at <u>www.</u> <u>ImpactStudentFinances.com</u> I interview my financial advisor and he discusses how you can build wealth from just $100 a month, over a period of time. What's amazing about this interview is that my financial advisor discusses how he began investing when he was only nineteen years old and now has a healthy nestegg that will allow him to comfortably have hundreds of thousands of dollars in the bank in his forties.

So in order to live on half of what you make, you must first figure out how much you need on a monthly basis to live an enjoyable and comfortable life. This number is called your financial number and it is very simple to calculate. Think about all the stuff that you have to pay for on a monthly basis. Not things your parents pay for, but rather things you have to pay for. If you are in high school this list should be very short, if you are in college, or out of college, it is a lot more detailed, but still very simple. Your financial number gives your money a job to do and it outlines a plan for that money. **Without a plan for your money it will not create wealth for you.**

Most high school students that don't have a job are given an allowance, holiday money, or birthday money. Either way, once you begin creating income make sure you have a plan developed to explain to your parents why they should continue to give you money for these things if they can afford to do so. When I was making money in my candy business in high school, I didn't have a plan for my money; therefore, just as quickly as I made it, I spent it.

If I would have known to spend half of what I made and put the other half aside, then my life would be very different. So again, look at what you spend money on, even if you do not have a means of income outside of your parents, think about why they give you money. Make a list of the things that your parents buy you on a monthly basis. Just in case you are drawing a blank, here is a list of some things the average parent gives the average high school student money for on a monthly basis:

Food

Clothes

Cell Phone

Gas (if you drive a car)

Outings with friends/Dating

For most high school students, this is a long list of monthly expenses. The only expenses I had in high school were the expenses I created for myself. **Don't create expenses that you do not need!** By living on half of what you make, you are building two very important skills as a young person: discipline and frugality. Calculate on average what your parents give you and/or what you make on a part-time job.

I reiterate: some of you reading this book may not have a consistent income and your parents probably only give you money on a need-to-have basis. That is irrelevant. That's where you are, not where you'll stay. If you activate some of the ideas outlined in this book you will have income very soon, but even if you don't do anything to obtain income, you will have income one day. Once that day comes, you need to do all that you can to live on half of what you make.

I understand that a lot of people have trouble believing they can build wealth and it takes a lot of work to change that, but much of what you are reading can be practiced now, even though you may not have a lot. Habits build wealth. Begin setting aside something from everything you get, even if it's $5 in a shoebox. **Remember: Habits build wealth.**

Next, after you have your financial number and you start putting a little bit of money away, you need to **get a bank account at an inconvenient bank and put all extra money in that account.**

An inconvenient bank is a bank where it would be very inconvenient for you or your guardian to withdraw money from. Inconvenient in this case means that: (1) It's not a bank that you can access online, (2) It's not connected to another account you use regularly, and (3) It's not physically located near you.

That means that it takes a lot of effort to get money out. **The best way to stay away from temptation is to keep it out of view.** If it's in view, you will always be tempted and even the most disciplined person falls to temptation sometimes, especially in matters of money. After you have your inconvenient bank account, then you want to start putting money inside of it.

Let's say you get $100 for Christmas money. Here is an example of how you could allocate that money. Tithe 10 percent (give to a church, favorite charity, or a person in need), in this example it would be $10. Then you have $90 left, automatically put half of that money ($45) in your inconvenient bank account. It may seem tough to do now, but if that doesn't seem like enough money then simply revisit Chapter 3 and find some ways to create more money via a job or a part-time business. If I were to propose this money management strategy to your parents, they would probably laugh at me and think I was crazy; well, you can do it easily with discipline and intelligence.

Finally, think ten years ahead from where you are now. This may be the toughest thing to do, but if you are going to be financially successful and, especially, if you are going to live on half of what you make, you have to think ahead. I wrote this book ten years ago and it seems like it was yesterday. Time flies whether you want to believe it or not.

My mentor often referred to the animal kingdom when he discussed finances; he always used to tell me to think like an ant. What he meant by this was: ants think ahead. Ants are working like crazy in the summer time thinking about the winter. They store up food for the winter during the summer months because they know once winter hits, they won't have any food if they don't.

You are in the "summer" season of your life. You are young, good looking, healthy, and intelligent, but you have to look ahead and understand that **if you don't make plans for the future you will plan to be a loser.** In ten years, how old will you be? Late-twenties, maybe? What do you want your life to look like?

Most people cannot live on half of what they make because they didn't discipline themselves when they were younger so now they are struggling. Don't struggle if you don't have to, live on half of what you make. If this is too impossible, start with living on 90 percent of what you make and just putting that 10 percent into an inconvenient bank account.

****

Chapter 4:
Things to Do

- Figure out how much money you spend on a monthly basis, if any.
- Open up an inconvenient bank account with your parent/guardian to put extra money away.
- Think like an ant. Use this summer of your life to plan and do things to get ahead.
- Sign up for the video series at **www.ImpactStudentFinances.com** and watch the video connected to this chapter.

CHAPTER 5:

Low Debt, High Credit

IT WAS A DARK, CLOUDY day when my mentor called and told me that our lesson was going to be a quick one, but he said it will be one of the most important ones. So I drove to his home enthralled with what the lesson could be. Once I arrived at his house, it began storming pretty bad and as I walked into his office, he said these words just as it thundered: "STAY OUT OF DEBT!" And that's how the lesson began. **Debt is like a drug, if you get hooked on it you can die financially.**

Is debt an absolute bad thing? No. Not if you properly manage debt, but as a teenager or college student, you will be given the opportunity to get into debt, do your best not to take these opportunities. Since I already had student loan debt when I began my mentorship, I was upset I hadn't received this message earlier, and if you already have debt, do not be discouraged, just take the lesson as I did, a reference for the future.

Your first debt should be a secured debt. Secured debt means that it is backed by cash you already have. Secured debt protects you in the event you cannot meet the monthly financial obligation. For example, let's say you have saved $500, and you get a secured credit card for $500. When you begin using that credit card, you will get a monthly bill. If it ends up you cannot pay, that $500 cash will pay the credit card off for you. So your debt is "secured" by your cash.

My mentor gave me three warnings about debt that you should heed:

Debt Warning #1 - Don't Ever Borrow What You Can't Afford

Most people graduate from college with over $30,000 in debt, with most of that debt being student loans. **<u>Do your very best not to ever get into student loan debt!</u>** These were the debts that got me behind in the beginning of my adult life. Student loans are a gamble that you will get a high paying job within a couple of years of graduation, which means you have already cut your salary.

I am connected with multiple organizations that help students find scholarships so they don't ever have to obtain debt and can avoid the plight I had. Make sure you sign up for our video series at www.ImpactStudentFinances.com.

There are literally millions left on the table each year by students who just don't put the work in to find scholarships. But if you have to get student loans, keep them as low as possible, always get federal loans, and don't borrow more than you believe you will make annually after you graduate.

For example, if the job you are shooting for is going to pay you $50,000 you should not go into more student loan debt than $50,000.

It would be better to go to community college and work to get scholarship money than get in a whole bunch of student loan debt. Most people end up changing their majors a lot anyway so you want to make sure you can go to school for free, or very inexpensively.

If you cannot afford a debt, do not get the debt. You will be approached by credit card companies and banks that want you to get a credit card with them or open an account. If you don't have a consistent source of income that can pay the debt and you can still live on half of your income then you do not need to get that debt.

That last line was so important I am going to actually type it again: **If you don't have a consistent source of income that can pay the debt and you can still live on half of your income after you pay the debt then you do not need to get that debt.**

Debt Warning #2 - Debt is Financial Slavery

I don't know what you believe, but I believe the Holy Bible, and it says in the Bible that the borrower is a servant to the lender (Proverbs 22:7). I just want to warn you that if you are deeply indebted, you are working for the person that you owe.

Let's say you owe $1,000 per month in debt and you make $2,000 per month, half of your paycheck is paying the people that you owe. So if you work six days a week, three of those days are working strictly to pay the debt that you owe. Make sure if you are a parent reading this book that you keep your children out of student loan debt. People say an education is priceless, that is false, they come with very large prices.

Debt Warning #3 - More Debt Now, Equals Less Money For You Later

A debt is something that you owe that you will one day pay off. The whole time you are paying a debt back you are using your hard earned money to satisfy that balance. If you stay out of debt you don't have to pay other people money. You can further invest in becoming wealthy. Keep most of your money by staying out of debt.

When you pay your home off you own the home, and historically homes go up in value. Even though that is the case, don't get caught in the trap: you have to have a thirty year mortgage, even if you owe on a home, pay it off as quickly as possible, do everything you can to stay out of bad debt completely. Keep your money, stay out of debt. Bad debt is debt that you pay off. There is such a thing as good debt. I talk about it more in our video series so make sure you sign up for it, but good debt is simply debt that pays for itself and then some.

An example of good debt is if you buy a house with a $100,000 mortgage and the monthly payment is $800 a month, but you rent that house out to someone else for $1500 a month. So you're in debt, but the money coming in is more than covering the debt. So in this example you're investing the debt and not just consuming the debt.

High Credit

In contrast to low debt, you must have high credit for financial success. What's interesting about the financial systems that are established in the United States is that you basically have to get into debt to build your credit. Your credit is built based upon four primary factors: your length of credit history, your payment history, your mix of credit, and your amount of debt.

Your credit score ranges from 300-850. Your credit score and profile is linked to your social security number. Your social security number is always linked to your credit. At this point in your life you probably do not use your credit much, but make your social security number sacred.

The only time you should share your social security number is if the college you are going to needs it or you need it for a bank account. **Don't give anybody your personal information, ever**, and even if you give it to them for the reasons I said before, ask a lot of questions. Treat your social security number like money, if someone asks for it, ask what they are using it for, who is going to see it, and any other questions you think of. We have a specific video attached to that which gives students credit tips to help them build impeccable credit.

If you keep your debt low and your credit high, it will be easier for you to become financially free!

****

Chapter 5:
Thing to Do

- If you're not in student loan debt, do your absolute best to never get any.
- Make sure you don't get into debt you can't afford.

- Watch our videos on debt and credit. If you haven't signed up to get the free videos that come along with this book, please visit: **www.ImpactStudentFinances.com**

CHAPTER 6:

Find What You Love to Do

THIS LESSON IS THE ONE that probably changed my life the most. It was a session where I was with some of my mentors' other students and hopefuls. He started one of his lectures that I initially thought had nothing to do with money.

"How many people do you think work jobs that they hate to make ends meet? Don't you know if you are stuck in a job that you don't love you will never have full satisfaction in life? Evangelist Shane Perry said, '*If you are stuck working a job that you hate, eventually you will hate your life.*' Go after what you love from this day on."

My parents told me to get a job that would pay me well and give me good benefits; my mentor told me that **perfected passion produces prosperity.** I don't know about you but I like what my mentor told me the best. Think about all the people that get paid tons of money, actors, athletes, entrepreneurs, and others. If you read their stories many of them started doing what they loved at an early age and became prosperous at a young age. People that do what they love usually make more money than those who don't do what they love.

This means that you should **identify what you love to do and then discover how you can get paid doing it**. In America, you can get paid for pretty much anything so why not get paid for what you love. My mentor called this thing your passion.

Your passion is something that you love to do so much that if money and time was no object you would continue doing it. Think hard about it, because it is very important. There are many ways to find your passion and I want to give you a few in this chapter.

The first way to find your passion is to look at what you do well. What comes to you naturally? What talents do you have? What do people say that you do well? Once you begin looking at these things you will discover your talents, many times your talents are tied to your passion.

Another way to discover your passion is by looking at what interests you. If you were to browse online for a book, which genre would you search for? Would you browse the science fiction section first, the business section, the carpentry section, or something else? Many times your passion is tied to your interests as well as your talents.

What are some things you talk about constantly? Think of conversations that you have with your friends, family, and loved ones. What movies do you like to watch? I am posing lots of questions to you to get your mind moving in the direction to find your passion. It is so important to do this and though your passion, directly, has nothing to do with dollars, once you find it, there are ways you can turn your passion into legitimate money making ventures.

The last way to find your passion is to look at the dreams and goals you have. Throughout this book I have mentioned writing down goals many times, refer to those goals and see if you can find something that you want to do that could be your passion. Your passion will keep you moving toward the achievement of your dreams and goals either because it is directly tied to those goals, or because you will be motivated to create a life so you can practice your passion on a regular basis.

After you discover what you love to do, it is just as pertinent to discover how to get paid for it. My mentor told me that if I could truly perfect my passion then I could produce enough prosperity to overcome any financial mistakes I made in the past. Hopefully you haven't made any financial mistakes thus far, but even if you have made some mistakes, discovering your passion will help you alleviate the negative impact of those mistakes.

With the emergence of social media more people are in tune with one of the most addictive phenomenons known to human-kind: Attention. The odd thing about getting attention is **most of the attention we seek is not profitable**. For the sake of this conversation, I want to stick to your ability to earn, save, and max-imize money. Getting the right type of attention can be profitable, but the likelihood of you getting profitable attention is low if you're general about your passion.

You must be very specific about what you're passionate about and who specifically it can serve. Read that again. Let's use a very general example and then a specific example. First, let's dis-cuss music. How can someone that is passionate about performing music serve other people? Initially they must pick a genre of music, get as good as they can with that genre, and consistently perform it. Be consistent about what you're doing and who you're doing it for.

A lot of people love music and are even good at performing it, but don't do well at being specific with what they're doing and who they're serving. Now for a more specific example. If someone was passionate about something that they're not good at, how could they serve? I'm going to get very specific here as it relates to sports, specifically basketball.

If you are passionate about basketball, but you're not good at it, how could you serve people? It's a question of what and who. Those that perform the sport well are serving the spectators' desire for entertainment. Since your lack of ability won't serve that purpose, you could help the actual athlete/performer do their work better. It's as simple as this: **"You're more likely to be like Rich Paul, than you are LeBron James."** In case you don't know, Rich Paul represents LeBron James as well as a lot of other professional athletes as their agent.

Said another way, no matter what you're passionate about, **if you learn how to market the interest or the performance of that thing, you'll always have creative ways to earn money.** This is critical beyond comprehension. When you find what you love to do and skillfully learn how to market what you love to do to others who love it, you can quietly build an amazing financial life.

Since I wrote the first edition of this book back in 2011 I've made hundreds of thousands of dollars speaking at multi-million dollar educational institutions, organizations, and groups all over the United States and Canada. A lot of people have paid me and told me that I am a really good speaker. The lightbulb came on for me, however, after 2018 when I started coaching other people to become professional speakers. I took my interest and passion as a professional speaker and began marketing as a speaking coach.

That has almost tripled my income in half the time.

The same thing can happen for you. Once you find your passion you must discover how you can get paid from it. This is where most people get it twisted. **What you do for a living defines who you are**.

Many people find what they love to do, but never discover how to get paid to do it. What you love to do and what you do well can serve well. Once you begin serving people, you will get paid. If you create a product, have a talent, or a particular skill that you are passionate about you can make money doing it. Some ways to do that is to look at other people who have the same passion or gifts that you do. There is an old saying, *"Don't reinvent the wheel, roll it to your success."* Don't copy what people do, copy how they do it.

Find people who do what you love to do and begin serving as they serve. If your passion is sports find out the many ways people get paid from your sport. If one of your passions is building things then see how you can get paid to build things. Make sure you don't get caught up in a job that you hate just to pay the bills. There is no honor in doing less than you are able to your whole life, and if you fail to plan, then you plan to fail. Plan to succeed in your passion and get to work perfecting it so you can create prosperity.

****

Chapter 6:
Things to Do

- Find out what you love to do, ask the questions to yourself and answer them.
- Figure out who you can serve.
- Visit **www.ImpactStudentFinances.com** and see the video on this particular chapter.

CHAPTER 7

Your Network Determines Your Net Worth

EVERYONE HAS HEARD THE SAYING, you learn something new everyday. While I had been studying under my mentor, I literally would learn something new every time he and I spoke. This particular lesson blew my mind because I really felt like this one lesson alone would take me to the top and I feel that way about you reading.

In fact, I'm going to go out on a limb and say if you implement what is in this one chapter, you'll never want for money ever again. This lesson is also the single most underrated and underutilized wealth building information known to man. So let me set the stage.

When I approached my mentor's office that morning he was on the phone, but motioned for me to come in nonetheless. Once he concluded the conversation, the lesson started.

"Odell, you've heard of Henry Ford haven't you?" he said while rustling some papers on his desk. "Yes, sir, he was the founder of Ford Motors," I said. "Correct! Did you know that Henry Ford had a sixth grade education and didn't make his first million until he was in his forties?"

"I didn't know that," I said.

"The reason why I mentioned Ford is because he was famous for his humility and his network. Ford worked for years on his own, perfecting his self-propelled carriage, but once he partnered with the right people the rest as they say, is history.

"It was only after he did that, he was able to go to another level in his business. The lesson is this, **it doesn't matter how much talent or intelligence you have, your network determines your net worth**." This lesson is about getting more of the right people in your life.

Write this down: **If tons of the right people know about you or know who you are in a favorable way, you will be successful.** Many times, if tons of people know you at all you will be very successful. The key word here is favorable. **Favor is better than fortune**. If people know that you do what you do well and they like you, then they will come to you before anybody else.

This is why it is so important to stay out of trouble and do right. People are more at ease when they know you do the right thing more often than not. All people, your family, friends, associates, and people in other networks have to know that you have integrity. Once they know this and trust this whenever you need something or want something they will be more inclined to give you what you need and/or want.

In high schools all over the world there are students that fit the description of a "teacher's pet." The teacher's pet is a student that the teacher *favors* over the other students for one reason or another.

In order for you to make your networks benefit you, you must obtain favor from the people you currently know, the people you will come to know, and by finding the right people to know.

The way you will obtain financial success earlier than later is by people purchasing goods and services from you on a consistent basis. The two key words you need to look at are "*people purchasing.*" If you look at the other chapters, I gave you tips to start creating money by starting part-time opportunities and jobs and saving money, but where is that money coming from? It is coming from people. Here's a great way to wealth: have something valuable to offer people you come in contact with. First, look at the people you currently know, like your friends, your family, your classmates, your teachers, and so on and so on.

These people I just mentioned already know you so why not obtain more favor with them by maintaining common courtesy, resolving conflicts, and maintaining a positive attitude. Also, evaluate the people you hang around regularly. Ask yourself these questions about your friends: 1) What kind of grades do my friends get? 2) Have my friends ever been to jail? 3) Do my friends go to church? 4) Do my friends have big goals they want to achieve later in life? 5) Are my "friends" really my friends? All of this may seem to be kind of pointless, but you do not need to have people in your network that decrease who you are.

The influence people have on you is either going to take you higher in life or take you down. Friends are like elevators, they either take you up or down and if you have a bunch of friends who are all about a good time and doing things that are not productive to your future, then you need to drop your friends. The friends you have now will not be your friends in the future because most of them are not going where you are going.

If you really want to increase your network's quality, be a high quality person. This doesn't mean that if something bad happens in your life you shouldn't show it, it just means that you have more days up than you do down. Attitude is more about how you look at things than how they really are. When faced with a tough situation, a good attitude gets you to always look on the bright side. If you don't think you can always look on the bright side, think of someone else who is worse off than you are. There is always someone worse off than you, trust me.

People love to be around people that have a positive attitude. People love to do business with people that have a positive attitude. People love to hire people with a positive attitude. So have a positive attitude as much as you possibly can.

Your bank account can be inflated or deflated because of who you know, but it can also be inflated or deflated by who knows you. Have you heard the saying, "It's not what you know, it's who you know"? Well there is a complimentary saying I want to give you as well, **"It's not who you know, but it's who knows who."**

Someone can favor you because of what they hear from somebody else. This is why it is so important to always be on your best behavior and have your best attitude. The people you will come to know could be CEOs of companies that will give you a job right out of school. The people you come to know could be that last contact you need before your book is sold to a big publisher. One thing the world has a great supply of is humans. Treat people right and let your passion be known to them, and they may possibly let you into their network.

Access into an affluent network can make a great impact on your life. Look at my life for example, I felt like I was on top of the world in college. My businesses on average were making about $1,000/month but I did not heed instructions because I was very prideful. Then once business started to slow down, I didn't know what to do. I ended up being broke right after college. That's when I started getting instruction from my mentor and then he began allowing me into his network of people and I have encountered a lot of success since then. What is equally important to always growing a great network is having solid mentors and trustworthy partners.

You must have a mentor in your network if you want to achieve financial success. Another key person you must have as your mentor is a spiritual guide. Not someone that is going to read scriptures to you everyday, but someone who can correct you when you are falling astray. Another key person you have to have in your network is a supporter, and you need many of those.

Supporters are people that don't actually *do* things per se to give you a profit or a benefit in what you are doing, but they make the event, they are there when you go to work, and get off. Supporters can come in the form of family, friends, or associates. The fact that you are young, a lot of people will gather around you and want to support you if you are doing something positive.

Just **remember that you are one contact away from living your dream life**. If someone sees you, hears about you, and the person with them can vouch for your integrity, you will be successful point blank. Your job is to expand your network. Make sure that the people you are currently attached to, or are in your network have a favorable opinion of you. Then understand that you will come across other people that you don't know that may know you.

Make a habit of adding mentors and supporters to the mix to help you reach for higher heights. Your networks determine your net worth, so make your networks large and make sure it is quality so it can serve you in the future!

I have an easy four step process for making profitable connections. I go deeper into it in the videos you have access to after you sign up but I want to share them very quickly.

Four Steps to Profitable Connections

First, do a great job at meeting the right people. The right people are those that can give you opportunities to earn more money. Even if you have no idea what you want to do when you get older, focus on being kind and developing an above average personality. If you happen to know what you want to do, make a habit of meeting the people in that industry.

The next thing you should do is build a connection with those individuals. I suggest that you use the FORM method to build an instant connection. FORM stands for:

F-family

O-occupation

R-recreation

M-motivation

No matter what stage of life you're in, you can connect one of these four things with a complete stranger. People connect to people they know, like, and trust. If you can build a connection by asking them about their family, their occupation (job/work/daily activity), their recreation (what they do for fun), and their motivation (why they do their work) then you can build a fast friend.

The third part to building profitable connections is to get their contact information. What's important about this step is to get an online way to contact them and an offline way. Emails and DMs on social media get lost in spam and are easily ignored. But if you have an offline way to contact someone, whether by phone or physical mail, it's more difficult to ignore.

The last part of profitable connecting is to **follow up with people and offer ways to be helpful in ways that are remarkable**. This is the life hack everybody wants to learn about. The vast majority of people do not follow up with people that they connect with. Most of the people that do follow up with ways to help in ways that are remarkable will be remembered. The more people that remember you in a favorable way the more likely they are to remember you when there are opportunities for you to be paid.

****

Chapter 7:
Things to Do

- Think of how you want to live and find people that live that way and connect with them.
- Seek mentors that will help you get to the next level. Try places like your school, books you read (hopefully me!),

Church, and other places.

- Connect with some of the mentors I interviewed. Get their contact information by logging into the portal found at **www.ImpactStudentFinances.com**.

CHAPTER 8:

Money is Only an Idea

ONE OF THE BIGGEST THINGS that my mentor instilled in me during my studies with him was that I could do anything. One of his favorite sayings was, "**Money is only an idea, and those who lack money simply lack ideas.**" My parents never seriously suggested to me that I come up with an idea to create a fortune.

My mentor always used to tell me over and over that I should come up with an idea to create a fortune. I suggest you work on that as well. It is my firm belief that people with high paying jobs are great at what they do, and just starting out you should strive to get the highest paying job you possibly can.

Once you get that job, however, you need to be doing your best to discover the idea that will make you a fortune. People always talk about the average person and not the person that realizes their potential and does something extraordinary. Extraordinary people read books like this as teenagers and young adults. Extraordinary people follow up with people and do things to stand out so that when an incredible scholarship or job opportunity comes up they are there to take full advantage.

Now, am I saying you will become a millionaire in your teens or twenties? It's possible, but not likely. But for those that have (outside of the ones who have rich relatives bank rolling them), they've come up with an extraordinary idea and implemented it. Spend time thinking, spend time creating a list of ideas you think can make you money. In fact, even if you are not in your twenties, a part of your day should be dedicated to developing an idea that will take your life to the next level.

Here's the biggest idea I want to submit to you: **Have a simple can't-miss financial plan and then always be working on a great business idea to create massive amounts of money**. This book has given you a great foundation on a simple can't-miss financial plan. Simply play Monopoly in real life. That "idea," is boring and requires discipline, but it's effective.

I want to hit a point home that my mentor always made sure he expressed to me: **You have the ability to live your dream life.** The ways you are going to live your dream life is by discovering what your dream life is, obtaining the money to pay for it, and then living it. Ideas from your imagination properly implemented will allow you to live your dreams, but the first part of that is to be sure to make a habit of creating ideas.

Albert Einstein said, "**Imagination is the preview of life's coming attractions**." Your ideas come from your imagination. If you take a look around the room you're in right now, all the things you see were created from someone's imagination.

You have an idea inside your mind right now that can create a dream life for you. What will it be? What is an idea that you have that can help people become more efficient? What is an idea that you have to make something people want, easier to obtain?

People will pay for ideas that make things more convenient for them. The cell phone was an extraordinary idea that did not create something new; it simply made an older idea (the landline telephone) easier to access. Now a cell phone is a necessity in our society. Before it was a luxury, now it is a necessity.

The founder of Facebook, Mark Zuckerberg, founded Facebook because he wanted students to be able to connect with their friends. That's it, that was the foundation of his idea. Look at Facebook now, that idea cashed in pretty well. Zuckerberg became a billionaire before the age of twenty-five off of one idea! Again, I don't want you to look at what these other people have done and feel like you have to become a billionaire in your twenties, but understand how great a developed idea can work for you.

To start finding ideas, look at what you are passionate about. Tony Robbins says, "**Passion is the genesis of genius.**" The things you are passionate about will allow you to develop ideas based on your strengths and talents. If the aforementioned young billionaire didn't know anything about computers or programming then his Facebook idea would've only been a pipe dream.

But if it's one thing I've learned in my life and business throughout the ten years that this book has been in publication is that **true innovation is making the best use of what's already here.** Most people don't ever find their true love in relationships or in work, not because they don't encounter it, but because they don't ask enough simple questions about what's mundane.

The idea of "wealth," comes from the desire to have more than what you need. How one can attain wealth is the quandary most people face. Be determined to make a strong income, be disciplined in how you handle that income, put your money in environments that it can reproduce over time consistently, and wait. I guarantee you will become wealthy eventually.

Pause right there and think about that idea. It's not innovative, sexy, or appealing. But it's easy to do. The idea of doing the right things to create wealth cannot get lost in translation. I am a huge proponent for abundance, massive success, and the power of positive thinking to produce amazing results. Nevertheless, I also know the value of discipline is understated. So again, let your first idea be to do the right things on a consistent basis.

When discovering the idea that is going to make you a fortune quicker than usual, look at the things you do well and things that you know before you develop the ideas. You have a lottery ticket inside of you and your idea is the winning number combination. If you are not actively trying to come up with ideas to obtain that winning number, then you might as well play the real lottery and waste your money. **You're one idea away from living like royalty.**

Beware of get-rich-quick scams and schemes that will surface as "good ideas." Understand that if you want to make money off of an idea, you have to know how that idea properly and legally gives value to other people in exchange for money. There are a lot of people out there who have ideas that fool and con people. I myself have seen firsthand what terrible people can do to naïve young people that are very ambitious.

Some of those people have ended up in jail, others have just been ruined financially. Do not let this happen to you! Come up with an authentic idea all of your own and make it profitable to you and allow it to bless the lives of others. Many ideas that people have come up with not only made them money, but most importantly saved people's lives both literally and figuratively.

Whose life are you going to save or help become better? The beautiful thing about a very good idea is that GOD allows the idea to bless the person that conceived it and the person that receives it. Walt Disney's idea was Mickey Mouse; now think of all the wonderful Disney movies and memories created at the theme parks all over the world. Bill Gates' idea was the personal computer and the vision of having one in every person's home.

Milton Hershey, the founder of the Hershey chocolate empire's idea was inexpensive quality chocolate. Though all these people had very different ideas, their ideas still bless people in so many ways. The world needs your ideas to help make it a better place, and you need your ideas to help you make some money so you can focus on the finer things in life.

****

Chapter 8:
Things to Do

- Understand that money is only an idea.
- The idea of being disciplined with money over time and investing is a radical idea.
- Find five people that inspire you to build a fortune and read their stories.
- Think of three things you would do for others once your idea makes you a fortune.

Never Give Up on Your Dreams

FINANCIAL SUCCESS IS VERY SUBJECTIVE. Some people want to make a million dollars in one year. Others just want to be debt free and build wealth steadily over time. My message to you in this book is simply no matter how you want to obtain wealth you can do it. You can live the life you want to live. A beautiful thing about being young is also one of the greatest disadvantages.

That thing is, when you are young you have yet to experience adulthood. Meaning you don't know what it's like to be older which can translate to a lackadaisical attitude about life because it seems like you have all the time in the world to frolic. But I will challenge you to develop powerful goals and develop a succinct plan to achieve your dreams while you are young.

Life is simple; just think about how you want to live when you are older. Find people that live that way and do what they did. It's that simple, **success leaves footprints, just follow them**. If you are a high school student and you want to have $10,000 saved by the time you are a college graduate, find someone who has $10,000 or more saved up and see how they did it. If your dream is bigger than that then you have to hang around people and learn from people that have done extraordinary things.

Though you may not achieve what they did in the exact same time frame, with intelligent and consistent diligence you can do big things in life. I want you to achieve financial greatness because money impacts everything in life. There are things more important than money, but if you have the level of financial success like I discussed in this book, you will be able to be free of financial pressure which will allow you to become a better citizen, parent, and family member.

The most important thing you have to do is never give up on going after financial achievement and personal success. Why not? Why not earn all you can, learn all you can, and give as much value as you can to the world? Look at all the people I have mentioned throughout the book who have done phenomenal things in their lives. Some were able to do it before thirty like Mark Zuckerberg with Facebook, but for most, it takes much longer, and that's okay.

The common theme between all of these individuals is that they never gave up on their dreams. They found their passions and continually forged ahead through the obstacles and setbacks. Both Walt Disney and Milton Hershey went through multiple bankruptcies before their businesses hit their peaks. So understand that financial achievement is something that will take hard work to attain.

I believe every person should go after the goal of financial achievement because becoming wealthy is not something that most people do. Since that is the case, you have to become better, learn more; become more disciplined, and more innovative to go attain that goal. Most people go to college and get their masters or their doctorate to receive more pay.

The reason why they get more pay is because they are reaching a level that most people don't ever go to. When you decide to make a goal to become wealthy, you will do the same thing. Again, I reiterate, don't ever give up on your dreams. Once you set your mind and your heart on what you want to achieve, promise yourself that you won't quit until you achieve it.

You were put here to win, not settle for less. Be excellent and use your excellence to bless others. Your contribution to this world may save a life, it may save a marriage, enhance something in this world to make the world better. If you give up on your dreams you may not be able to make the same contribution.

My parents didn't tell me the eight things in this book because they didn't know. I was able to learn these things by trial and error and through mentorship. As we conclude this book I want to leave you four things to expect so you never give up on your dreams:

Expect Greatness — Know that you were sent to this world to make an impact on people in a positive way and in your destiny is all that you need to prosper. Expect to be great; don't settle for being an ornament when you've got what it takes to be the star.

Expect Opposition — Know that the greater your dream, the greater the opposition. If you want to be wealthy, know that more people/circumstances/trials will come your way to hinder you than if you choose to settle for financial mediocrity. Don't run from opposition, run toward it and conquer it.

Expect to Grow — Understand that in order for you to have more, you must grow to be able to hold it all. Expect you will have to learn a skill, trade, or some sort of information that is going to take you to the top.

Expect to Pay — Know that you have to pay your dues. The greater the feat in which you want to accomplish, the greater the price. You never get something for nothing in this life, don't expect it. Expect that your wealth will come with a price, expect that your happiness will come with a price, because it will. Just note that **the price for success costs way less than the price of failure**. Don't be cheap about your future, pay in advance and in full.

Now that you have these things in this short book use them to augment everything you do in school, work, and life. GOD bless you and I wish you a great life, both personally and financially.

****

Don't forget to get your free video series at **www.ImpactStudentFinances.com** *and check out* some of our interviews.

#1 Thing to Do:
Know that Financial Success is Your Duty

AFTER READING THIS BOOK, I want you to understand that there are only a few things you need to do for maximum impact. So many people believe that there are a lot of things you have to do to be happy. That being said, the first thing you have to do is know in your heart, mind, and soul that it is your duty to be a financial success in life. I was first introduced to this concept by Russell Conwell.

He was the founder of Temple University and was a preacher who began preaching about prosperity a very long time ago. As we have discussed, you can do a lot more good with lots of money than you can without it. So after reading this book, the first thing I need you to do is know that financial success is your duty. Many people don't become wealthy and financially successful because they don't place much value on doing so.

Place TONS of value on becoming financially successful. Make it just as necessary as becoming a high school or college graduate!

#2 Thing to Do:
Start Saving to Play Monopoly

WE TALKED ABOUT EARNING INCOME in great detail in Chapter 3. Very simply, after you read this book I want you to focus on playing Monopoly in real life. Live on half of the income you earn from a job and with the rest of the money, save it to develop the habit of saving money for a purpose.

The hope is to purchase assets later in life. Hoard money for the purpose of purchasing assets. An asset is anything you own or control that produces money for you with little or none of your involvement.

In Monopoly, you purchase real estate and businesses to produce money for you. In real life, you should be looking to do much of the same. Look at the ideas listed in Chapter 3. Hopefully these ideas will get the wheels in your head turning in the direction of obtaining money. For now, save your money. My mentor always used to tell me that if you save your money long enough someone will come along to show you how to double it.

#3 Thing to Do:
Continually Invest in Yourself

You HAVE TO INVEST IN yourself to become successful financially. It's not an option, it's a prerequisite. You should be buying at least five books a year. After you buy them, read them and study them. Along with buying five books, invest in yourself by purchasing at least two audio programs a year and consider this program as one of your purchases.

Also take classes, go to seminars, and get educated anyway you can. Learn something that will allow you to increase your earning potential and learn how to buy assets.

#4 Thing to Do:
Associate with the Right People

THE NUMBER ONE ROOT CAUSE **of a mediocre financial life is an association with the wrong people**. Your associations determine how you live. Just choose to associate with the right friends, mentors, and groups or organizations. Your ability to do this will move you so far ahead, your life will never be the same. Remember, if you want to be a millionaire, get some millionaire friends. If you want to be mediocre, get mediocre friends. Who you hang around and allow in your life determines whether or not you're mediocre financially or a millionaire.

The Obligatory End of Book Picture

This is the end of the book, so I'm supposed to put my picture here!

For More Information and Resources

VISIT

www.ImpactStudentFinances.com

Made in the USA
Monee, IL
19 April 2021

65140712R00056